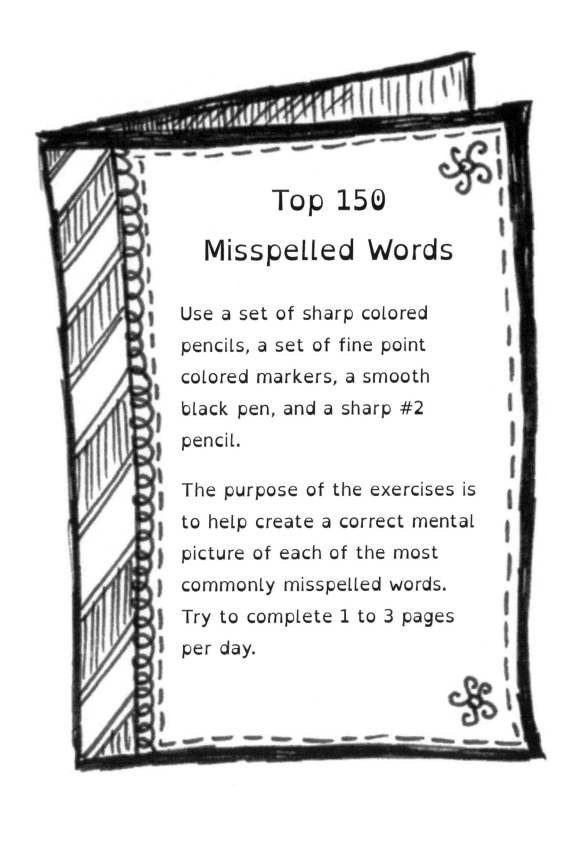

Top 150
Misspelled Words

Use a set of sharp colored pencils, a set of fine point colored markers, a smooth black pen, and a sharp #2 pencil.

The purpose of the exercises is to help create a correct mental picture of each of the most commonly misspelled words. Try to complete 1 to 3 pages per day.

The TOP 150 Commonly Misspelled Words

1. absence	39. convenience	77. independent	115. principal
2. acceptable	40. criticize	78. intelligence	116. principle
3. accidentally	41. describe	79. interesting	117. privilege
4. accommodate	42. decide	80. island	118. pronunciation
5. across	43. deceive	81. jealous	119. publicly
6. achieve	44. definite	82. jewelry	120. questionnaire
7. acquire	45. definitely	83. judgment	121. quiet
8. advertise	46. develop	84. kernel	122. realize
9. advice	47. discipline	85. knowledge	123. receive
10. adult	48. does	86. leisure	124. receipt
11. a lot	49. during	87. lesson	125. recommend
12. almost	50. easily	88. liaison	126. referred
13. amateur	51. eight	89. liberty	127. reference
14. among	52. either	90. library	128. relevant
15. annually	53. embarrass	91. license	129. restaurant
16. apparent	54. equipment	92. lying	130. rhyme
17. argument	55. exhilarate	93. maintenance	131. rhythm
18. awful	56. exceed	94. maneuver	132. safety
19. balance	57. excellent	95. marriage	133. schedule
20. becoming	58. exercise	96. medieval	134. scissors
21. before	59. existence	97. millennium	135. separate
22. believe	60. experience	98. miniature	136. speech
23. breathe	61. familiar	99. minute	137. surprise
24. brilliant	62. finally	100. mischievous	138. their
25. business	63. foreign	101. misspell	139. they're
26. burglar	64. forty	102. neighbor	140. there
27. calendar	65. friend	103. noticeable	141. toward
28. careful	66. government	104. occasion	142. truly
29. category	67. grammar	105. occasionally	143. twelfth
30. changeable	68. grateful	106. occurrence	144. until
31. citizen	69. guarantee	107. official	145. unusual
32. collectible	70. happiness	108. often	146. usually
33. column	71. harass	109. paid	147. vacuum
34. coming	72. height	110. perform	148. village
35. committed	73. heroes	111. perseverance	149. weather
36. competition	74. humorous	112. picture	150. weird
37. conscience	75. ignorance	113. possession	
38. conscious	76. immediate	114. precede	

Add Colors to Each Word:

1. ABSENCE
2. ACCEPTABLE
3. ACCIDENTALLY
4. ACCOMMODATE
5. ACROSS
6. ACHIEVE
7. ACQUIRE
8. ADVERTISE
9. ADVICE

Fill in the Missing Letters:

1. ABSENCE	1. a en e
2. ACCEPTABLE	2. a ept le
3. ACCIDENTALLY	3. ac ent ly
4. ACCOMMODATE	4. ac mo te
5. ACROSS	5. a o s
6. ACHIEVE	6. ach e
7. ACQUIRE	7. a ui e
8. ADVERTISE	8. ad rt e
9. ADVICE	9. a vi e
10. ADULT	10. a lt
11. A LOT	11. a t
12. ALMOST	12. a st
13. AMATEUR	13. am r
14. AMONG	14. a ng
15. ANNUALLY	15. an l y
16. APPARENT	16. ap r nt
17. ARGUMENT	17. ar m nt
18. AWFUL	18. a l

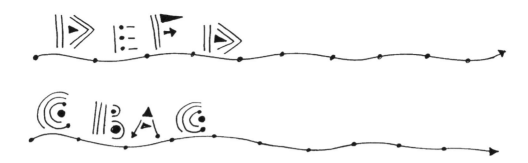

Add Colors to Each Word:

1. ADULT
2. A LOT
3. ALMOST
4. AMATEUR
5. AMONG
6. ANNUALLY
7. APPARENT
8. ARGUMENT
9. AWFUL

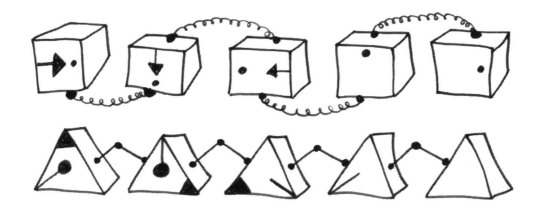

Fill in the Missing Letters:

1. absence	1. ab___ce	1. ab_____
2. acceptable	2. a___ptable	2. ac_____e
3. accidentally	3. ac___entally	3. ac_____ly
4. accommodate	4. accom___ate	4. ac_____te
5. across	5. ac___s	5. a____s
6. achieve	6. ac___ve	6. a_____e
7. acquire	7. a___ire	7. a_____e
8. advertise	8. adver___e	8. a_____e
9. advice	9. ad___e	9. a____e
10. adult	10. a__lt	10. a____
11. a lot	11. a l__	11. a ___
12. almost	12. al___t	12. a____t
13. amateur	13. ama___r	13. a_____r
14. among	14. a___g	14. a____
15. annually	15. a___ally	15. an_____
16. apparent	16. ap___ent	16. ap_____
17. argument	17. arg___nt	17. ar_____
18. awful	18. a___l	18. a____

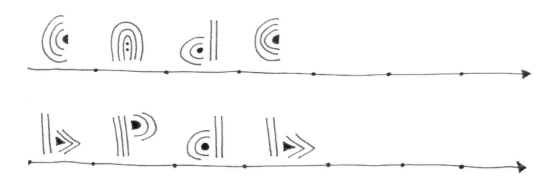

Add Colors to Each Word:

1. BALANCE
2. BECOMING
3. BEFORE
4. BELIEVE
5. BREATHE
6. BRILLIANT
7. BUSINESS
8. BURGLAR

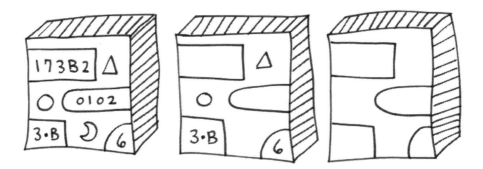

Write in the Missing Words or Letters:

1. BALANCE	1. BAL NCE
2. BECOMING	2.
3. BEFORE	3. BEFO E
4. BELIEVE	4.
5. BREATHE	5. BR ATHE
6. BRILLIANT	6.
7. BUSINESS	7. BUSINE S
8. BURGLAR	8. BU GLAR
9. CALENDAR	9.
10. CAREFUL	10. CAR FUL
11. CATEGORY	11.
12. CHANGEABLE	12. CHANGE BLE
13. CITIZEN	13.
14. COLLECTIBLE	14. COLLECT LE
15. COLUMN	15. COL N
16. COMING	16.
17. COMMITTED	17. COM IT ED
18. COMPETITION	18.
19. CONSCIENCE	19. CONSC NCE
20. CONSCIOUS	20. CO SC US
21. CONVENIENCE	21.
22. CRITICIZE	22. CRIT CI E

Add Colors to Each Word:

1. CALENDAR
2. CAREFUL
3. CATEGORY
4. CHANGEABLE
5. CITIZEN
6. COLLECTIBLE
7. COLUMN
8. COMING
9. COMMITTED
10. COMPETITION

11. CONSCIENCE
12. CONSCIOUS
13. CONVENIENCE
14. CRITICIZE

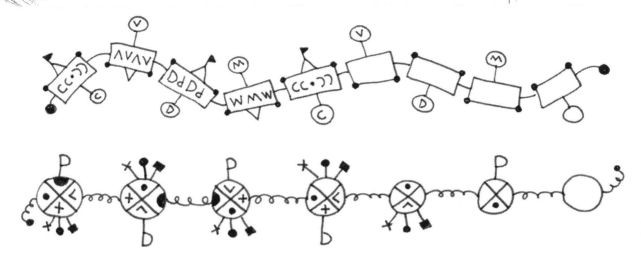

Write in the Missing Words:

#		#		#
1.	balance	1.	balance	1. _____
2.	becoming	2.	becoming	2. _____
3.	before	3.	before	3. _____
4.	believe	4.	believe	4. _____
5.	breathe	5.	breathe	5. _____
6.	brilliant	6.	brilliant	6. _____
7.	business	7.	business	7. _____
8.	burglar	8.	burglar	8. _____
9.	calendar	9.	calendar	9. _____
10.	careful	10.	careful	10. _____
11.	category	11.	category	11. _____
12.	changeable	12.	changeable	12. _____
13.	citizen	13.	citizen	13. _____
14.	collectible	14.	collectible	14. _____
15.	column	15.	column	15. _____
16.	coming	16.	coming	16. _____
17.	committed	17.	committed	17. _____
18.	competition	18.	competition	18. _____
19.	conscience	19.	conscience	19. _____
20.	conscious	20.	conscious	20. _____
21.	convenience	21.	convenience	21. _____
22.	criticize	22.	criticize	22. _____

 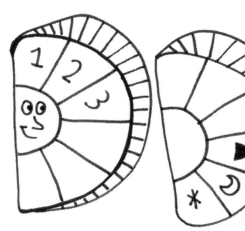 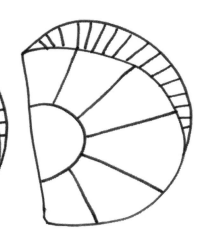

Add Colors to Each Word:

1. DESCRIBE
2. DECIDE
3. DECEIVE
4. DEFINITE
5. DEFINITELY
6. DEVELOP
7. DISCIPLINE
8. DOES
9. DURING

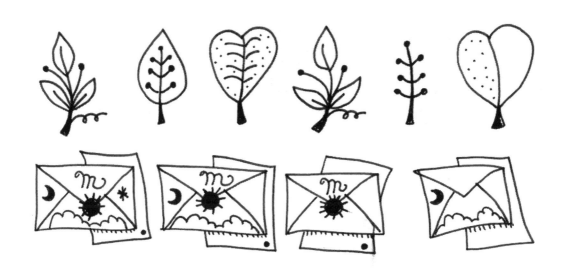

Fill in the Missing Letters:

1.	DESCRIBE	1.	DES RI E
2.	DECIDE	2.	DE I E
3.	DECEIVE	3.	DE E VE
4.	DEFINITE	4.	DE IN TE
5.	DEFINITELY	5.	DE IN T LY
6.	DEVELOP	6.	D VE OP
7.	DISCIPLINE	7.	DI CI L NE
8.	DOES	8.	DO S
9.	DURING	9.	D R NG
10.	EASILY	10.	E S LY
11.	EIGHT	11.	E G T
12.	EITHER	12.	E TH R
13.	EMBARRASS	13.	EMB RR SS
14.	EQUIPMENT	14.	EQ IPM NT
15.	EXHILARATE	15.	EXH L R TE
16.	EXCEED	16.	EXC ED
17.	EXCELLENT	17.	EXC LL NT
18.	EXERCISE	18.	EX RC SE
19.	EXISTENCE	19.	EX ST NCE
20.	EXPERIENCE	20.	EXP R ENCE

Add Colors to Each Word:

1. EASILY
2. EIGHT
3. EITHER
4. EMBARRASS
5. EQUIPMENT
6. EXHILARATE
7. EXCEED
8. EXCELLENT
9. EXERCISE
10. EXISTENCE
11. EXPERIENCE

Write in the Missing Words:

1.	1. DESCRIBE	1. describe
2. decide	2.	2. decide
3. deceive	3. DECEIVE	3.
4.	4. DEFINITE	4. definite
5. definitely	5.	5. definitely
6. develop	6. DEVELOP	6.
7.	7. DISCIPLINE	7. discipline
8. does	8.	8. does
9. during	9. DURING	9.
10.	10. EASILY	10. easily
11. eight	11.	11. eight
12. either	12. EITHER	12.
13.	13. EMBARRASS	13. embarrass
14. equipment	14.	14. equipment
15. exhilarate	15. EXHILARATE	15.
16.	16. EXCEED	16. exceed
17. excellent	17.	17. excellent
18. exercise	18. EXERCISE	18.
19.	19. EXISTENCE	19. existence
20. experience	20.	20. experience

G H I G

J K L J

Add Colors to Each Word:

1. FAMILIAR
2. FINALLY
3. FOREIGN
4. FORTY
5. FRIEND
6. GOVERNMENT
7. GRAMMAR
8. GRATEFUL
9. GUARANTEE

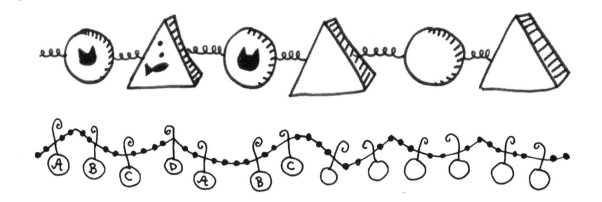

Add Colors to Each Word:

1. HAPPINESS
2. HARASS
3. HEIGHT
4. HEROES
5. HUMOROUS
6. IGNORANCE
7. IMMEDIATE
8. INDEPENDENT
9. INTELLIGENCE
10. INTERESTING
11. ISLAND

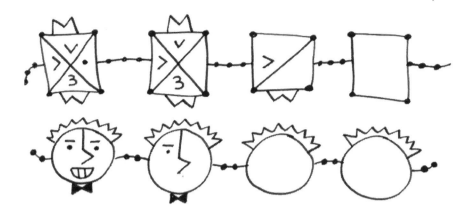

Fill in the Missing Letters:

1. familiar	1. famil ar	1. fa ar
2. finally	2. f nally	2. f ly
3. foreign	3. fore gn	3. fo n
4. forty	4. f rty	4. f y
5. friend	5. fri nd	5. f nd
6. government	6. gov rnm nt	6. gover nt
7. grammar	7. gr mm r	7. gram r
8. grateful	8. gr t ful	8. gr ful
9. guarantee	9. gu r nt e	9. gua tee
10. happiness	10. h pp n ss	10. hap ess
11. harass	11. h r ss	11. ha s
12. height	12. he ght	12. h ht
13. heroes	13. hero s	13. he s
14. humorous	14. hum ro s	14. hum us
15. ignorance	15. ign r nce	15. ignor e
16. immediate	16. imm di te	16. i diate
17. independent	17. ind p nd nt	17. inde dent
18. intelligence	18. int ll g nce	18. in nce
19. interesting	19. int r st ng	19. int ing
20. island	20. i l nd	20. i d

Add Colors to Each Word:

1. JEALOUS
2. JEWELRY
3. JUDGMENT
4. KERNEL
5. KNOWLEDGE
6. LEISURE
7. LESSON
8. LIAISON
9. LIBERTY
10. LIBRARY
11. LICENSE
12. LYING

Fill in the Missing Vowels:

1. jealous
2. jewelry
3. judgment
4. kernel
5. knowledge
6. leisure
7. lesson
8. liaison
9. liberty
10. library
11. license
12. lying

1. j   l   s
2. j   w   lry
3. j   dgm   nt
4. k   rn   l
5. kn   wl   dg
6. l   s   r
7. l   ss   n
8. l   s   n
9. l   b   rty
10. l   br   ry
11. l   c   ns
12. ly   ng

Add Colors to Each Word:

1. MAINTENANCE
2. MANEUVER
3. MARRIAGE
4. MEDIEVAL
5. MILLENNIUM
6. MINIATURE
7. MINUTE
8. MISCHIEVOUS
9. MISSPELL

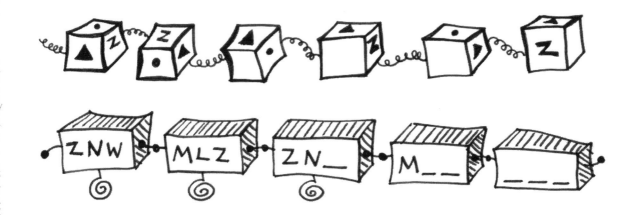

Fill in the Missing Vowels:

1. maintenance	1. m nt n nc
2. maneuver	2. m n v r
3. marriage	3. m rr g
4. medieval	4. m d v l
5. millennium	5. m ll nn m
6. miniature	6. m n t r
7. minute	7. m n t
8. mischievous	8. m sch v s
9. misspell	9. m ssp ll

Add Colors to Each Word:

1. NEIGHBOR
2. NOTICEABLE
3. OCCASION
4. OCCASIONALLY
5. OCCURRENCE
6. OFFICIAL
7. OFTEN

Write in the Missing Words:

1. NEIGHBOR	1.	1. neighbor
2. NOTICEABLE	2. noticeable	2.
3. OCCASION	3.	3. occasion
4. OCCASIONALLY	4. occasionally	4.
5. OCCURRENCE	5.	5. occurrence
6. OFFICIAL	6. official	6. official
7. OFTEN	7.	7. often
8. PAID	8. paid	8.
9. PERFORM	9.	9. perform
10. PERSEVERANCE	10. perseverance	10.
11. PICTURE	11.	11. picture
12. POSSESSION	12. possession	12.
13. PRECEDE	13.	13. precede
14. PRINCIPAL	14.	14. principal
15. PRINCIPLE	15. principle	15.
16. PRIVILEGE	16.	16. privilege
17. PRONUNCIATION	17. pronunciation	17.
18. PUBLICLY	18.	18. publicly

Add Colors to Each Word:

1. PAID
2. PERFORM
3. PERSEVERANCE
4. PICTURE
5. POSSESSION
6. PRECEDE
7. PRINCIPAL
8. PRINCIPLE
9. PRIVILEGE
10. PRONUNCIATION
11. PUBLICLY

Add Colors to Each Word:

1. QUIET
2. REALIZE
3. RECEIVE
4. RECEIPT
5. RECOMMEND
6. REFERRED
7. REFERENCE
8. RELEVANT
9. RESTAURANT
10. RHYME
11. RHYTHM

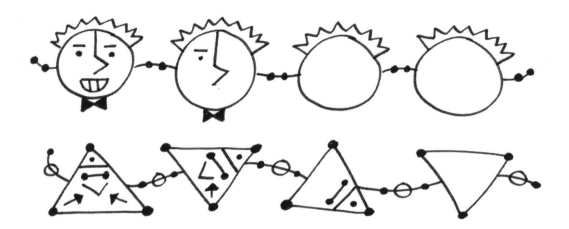

Fill in the Missing Vowels:

1.	quiet	1. qu t
2.	realize	2. r l z
3.	receive	3. r c v
4.	receipt	4. r c pt
5.	recommend	5. r c mm nd
6.	referred	6. r f rr d
7.	reference	7. r f r nc
8.	relevant	8. r l v nt
9.	restaurant	9. r st r nt
10.	rhyme	10. rh m
11.	rhythm	11. rh thm
12.	safety	12. s f ty
13.	schedule	13. sch d l
14.	scissors	14. sc ss rs
15.	separate	15. s p r t
16.	speech	16. sp ch
17.	surprise	17. s rpr s

Add Colors to Each Word:

1. SAFETY
2. SCHEDULE
3. SCISSORS
4. SEPARATE
5. SPEECH
6. SURPRISE

Add Colors to Each Word:

1. THEIR
2. THEY'RE
3. THERE
4. TOWARD
5. TRULY
6. TWELFTH

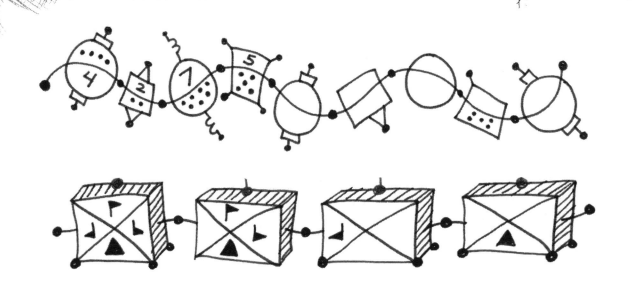

Fill in the Missing Letters:

1. TH R	1. THEIR	1. T R
2. TH 'RE	2. THEY'RE	2. T 'RE
3. TH RE	3. THERE	3. T E
4. TO RD	4. TOWARD	4. T D
5. TR Y	5. TRULY	5. T Y
6. T LFTH	6. TWELFTH	6. T H
7. UN L	7. UNTIL	7. U L
8. U SUAL	8. UNUSUAL	8. U L
9. USU LY	9. USUALLY	9. U Y
10. VA UM	10. VACUUM	10. V M
11. V LAGE	11. VILLAGE	11. V E
12. WE HER	12. WEATHER	12. W R
13. W RD	13. WEIRD	13. W D

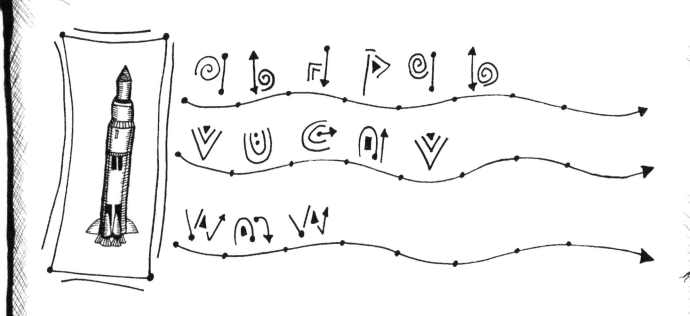

Add Colors to Each Word:

1. UNTIL
2. UNUSUAL
3. USUALLY
4. VACUUM
5. VILLAGE
6. WEATHER
7. WEIRD

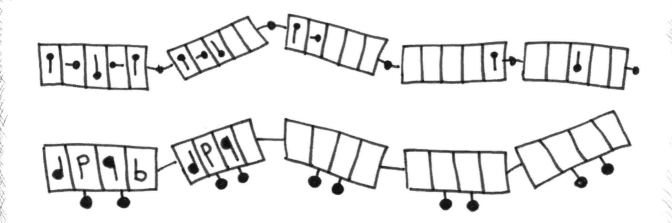

Write in the Missing Words:

1. their
2. _____
3. there
4. _____
5. truly
6. _____
7. until
8. _____
9. usually
10. _____
11. village
12. _____
13. weird

1. _____
2. they're
3. _____
4. toward
5. _____
6. twelfth
7. _____
8. unusual
9. _____
10. vacuum
11. _____
12. weather
13. _____

Use this page to practice writing these words.

1. absence
2. acceptable
3. accidentally
4. accommodate
5. across
6. achieve
7. acquire
8. advertise
9. advice
10. adult

Absence ACQUIRE
Acceptable Across
Accidentally
ACHIEVE
Advertise Advice
Almost

Use this page to practice writing these words.

1. a lot
2. almost
3. amateur
4. among
5. annually
6. apparent
7. argument
8. awful

Use this page to practice writing these words.

1. balance
2. becoming
3. before
4. believe
5. breathe
6. brilliant
7. business
8. burglar

Use this page to practice writing these words.

1. calendar
2. careful
3. category
4. changeable
5. citizen
6. collectible
7. column
8. coming
9. committed
10. competition
11. conscience
12. conscious

Use this page to practice
writing these words.

1. describe
2. decide
3. deceive
4. definite
5. definitely
6. develop
7. discipline
8. does
9. during

Use this page to practice writing these words.

1. easily
2. eight
3. either
4. embarrass
5. equipment
6. exhilarate
7. exceed
8. excellent
9. exercise
10. existence
11. experience

Use this page to practice writing these words.

1. familiar
2. finally
3. foreign
4. forty
5. friend
6. government
7. grammar
8. grateful
9. guarantee
10. happiness
11. harass
12. height

Use this page to practice
writing these words.

1. ignorance
2. immediate
3. independent
4. intelligence
5. interesting
6. island
7. jealous
8. jewelry
9. judgment
10. kernel
11. knowledge

Use this page to practice
writing these words.

1. leisure
2. lesson
3. liaison
4. liberty
5. library
6. license
7. lying

Use this page to practice writing these words.

1. maintenance
2. maneuver
3. marriage
4. medieval
5. millennium
6. miniature
7. minute
8. mischievous
9. misspell

Use this page to practice
writing these words.

1. neighbor
2. noticeable
3. occasion
4. occasionally
5. occurrence
6. official
7. often
8. paid
9. perform

Use this page to practice writing these words.

1. perseverance
2. picture
3. possession
4. precede
5. principal
6. principle
7. privilege
8. pronunciation
9. publicly

Use this page to practice writing these words.

1. quiet
2. realize
3. receive
4. receipt
5. recommend
6. referred
7. reference
8. relevant
9. restaurant
10. rhyme
11. rhythm

Use this page to practice
writing these words.

1. safety
2. schedule
3. scissors
4. separate
5. speech
6. surprise
7. their
8. they're
9. there
10. toward

Use this page to practice writing these words.

1. truly
2. twelfth
3. until
4. unusual
5. usually
6. vacuum
7. village
8. weather
9. weird

Use this page to practice writing these words.

1. a lot
2. almost
3. amateur
4. among
5. annually
6. apparent
7. argument
8. awful

Use this page to practice writing these words.

1. a lot
2. almost
3. amateur
4. among
5. annually
6. apparent
7. argument
8. awful